"A window. A whole of life already framed.
Right there. A bird whizzing by, a bumblebee.
Always different."

—Maud Lewis

To my dear friend Nan Forler,
who reminds me—as Maud has done through her art—
to find beauty in the everyday. —K.S.

For Nana Mona and her rambling, rowdy,
and big-hearted family, the Gouldens. —L.S.

Text copyright © 2023 by Kathy Stinson
Illustrations copyright © 2023 by Lauren Soloy

23 24 25 26 27 5 4 3 2 1

Greystone Kids / Greystone Books Ltd.
greystonebooks.com

Cataloging data available from Library and Archives Canada
ISBN 978-1-77164-951-3 (cloth)
ISBN 978-1-77164-952-0 (epub)

Editing by Kallie George
Copy editing by Doretta Lau
Proofreading by Doeun Rivendell
Jacket and interior design by Sara Gillingham Studio
Disability awareness review by Karen Autio

Printed and bound in China on FSC® certified paper by Shenzhen Reliance Printing.
The FSC® label means that materials used for the product have been responsibly sourced.
The illustrations in this book were rendered digitally with an iPad and pencil.

Greystone Books thanks the Canada Council for the Arts, the British Columbia Arts Council,
the Province of British Columbia through the Book Publishing Tax Credit, and the Government
of Canada for supporting our publishing activities.

Canada

Greystone Books gratefully acknowledges the xʷməθkʷəy̓əm (Musqueam),
Sḵwx̱wú7mesh (Squamish), and səl̓ílwətaʔɬ (Tsleil-Waututh) peoples on
whose land our Vancouver head office is located.

A TULIP IN WINTER

A Story About Folk Artist Maud Lewis

Kathy Stinson
+
Lauren Soloy

GREYSTONE KIDS

GREYSTONE BOOKS • VANCOUVER/BERKELEY/LONDON

Close to a highway sat a little house
like others in Nova Scotia.

And *not* like others.

Birds and butterflies danced
up and down its door
and flowers were painted on its window!

Who would do such a thing?

A woman as one-of-a-kind
as her house!

When Maud was a child, she was happy
playing with her brother,
watching her father make harnesses in his blacksmith shop,
and on family outings along the shore.

Other children teased her
for how she looked,
her crooked walk,
and how small she was.

Her doctor could not
explain her condition.

Still, at home Maud was content,
stroking the cats,
listening to music,
and playing piano.

But as her hands grew more bent
and her fingers more stiff,
sweet music turned sour.

"I can't do this!" Maud banged on the keys.

"Come," her mother said.
"Let's see if you can hold a paintbrush."

Maud jabbed the brush into red
and dragged it across the paper.

"Oh!"

Red on white
made its own kind of music.

Maud dipped the brush again.
Gently this time.

"Look! I made a flower!"

Maud began making Christmas cards
with her mother.

She began noticing:
Pictures on calendars and cookie tins.
Eyelashes on massive oxen.
The reflection of a boat on water.
The curve of a butterfly wing.

Shapes.
Lines.
Colours.
Everywhere!

As Maud grew up, colour flowed through her days.

But as an adult, hardship visited her again and again.

She tried to get a job. Store owners shook their heads.
Could they not see she was as capable of serving customers
as other young women?

When her parents died, her brother sold their house and moved away.

Penniless, Maud had to move in with her aunt.

"You can't paint in here," Aunt Ida said. "Too messy."

Maud went to the porch.

"Not here either. You should learn to crochet instead."

Do this. Don't do that. Do this. Don't do that.

Maud needed a home where she would be treated like an adult and accepted for who she was.

Her cousin said, "I hear the fish peddler
is looking for a live-in housekeeper."

Far along the highway Maud trudged,
her ankles aching.

The fish peddler, Everett Lewis, was as gruff as a billy goat,
his house as dreary as a dishpan of dirty water.

"This, what you've got—is it contagious?"
"No."
"Alright then."

Right away Maud began adding touches
of colour to the dull little house,
humming happily to herself.

Sadly, when her paint supplies ran out,
there was no money for more.

Everett knew what to do.

Off to the dump he went
for scraps of wood and cardboard,
and to the wharf where fishermen painted their boats,
to collect what was left over.

At the beach he strode into the waves
to fetch a can bobbing close to shore.

At home Maud peeled back the dry layer of paint
to get at the fresh paint underneath.

Everett was strong in body.
Maud was strong in spirit.
They got along the way certain colours do.

Together, as man and wife, they drove around the countryside,
selling Everett's fish and Maud's creations—
until he had to sell the car
because it cost too much to run.

Sometimes customers and friends gave Maud gifts of paint.
Sometimes, when there was enough money, Everett did too.

Days could be white with snow or grey with fog,
but inside Maud the sun was shining
as she squeezed bright yellow into a sardine tin.

She dipped her brush in blue
and heard waves lapping the shore.

Maud painted old times, happy times,
village, country, and seaside scenes,
and all the beauty she had ever seen in nature.

She painted on walls,
windows, doors, shelves,
trays, breadboxes, tea canisters,
the dustpan . . .

Even the woodstove!

People often stopped at the one-of-a-kind house to look or buy a painting.

"Such a cheerful scene!"

"Reminds me of days gone by."

"Her paintings are all so joyous!"

Maud was happy seeing her work give others such pleasure.

A woman said to her, "Your cats among the tulips are delightful."

Behind that customer was a child peeking out.

Maud smiled. The child smiled back.

After a time, Maud was in too much pain to walk
or even to paint.

Everett carried Maud to his wheelbarrow.
He pushed it to where she could see the sweet peas blooming.
"Thank you, Ev," she said.

Maud was looking past what was hard,
seeing what was good and beautiful,
as she had all her life—
and would until the end.

So small was Maud that she was buried in a child's coffin.

So small was her house that it is now nestled inside the Art Gallery of Nova Scotia.

But the effect of the joyous art this little one-of-a-kind woman created in the little one-of-a-kind house by the highway?

Enormous!

About Maud Lewis

Maud Lewis was born Maud Dowley on March 7, 1903, in Yarmouth, Nova Scotia. The physical condition that made her appear different as a child developed into severe and painful rheumatoid arthritis. What truly made Maud different was her unique ability to see beauty in the everyday, despite the many hardships she faced, and her talent for capturing all she found beautiful in her joyful, exuberant art.

Maud never attended art school or visited an art gallery. She brought a natural ability for using colour, shape, and line to her compositions, in ways that gave them a cheerful energy and sense of movement.

She brought a gentle sense of humour to her work too. If there is snow on the ground, mountaintops are not green—except in Maud's paintings. And if she felt like putting spring blossoms or autumn leaves in a winter scene, she did. Smiling, Maud said, "I like to put in what's pretty about all seasons."

Was Everett miserly and cruel, as some people believe, because he never spent money—even when he had it—on things that would have made the house more comfortable for Maud? Things like electricity, a screen door, and indoor plumbing? Or was Everett simply content with how things were, or afraid of spending money because of his poor background?

Whatever the case, Everett did make it possible for Maud to pursue her passion for painting, and she relieved him of a deep loneliness.

Maud died on July 30, 1970. By the time Everett died nine years later, the house on the highway was in rough shape. Its wood was rotting, its plaster crumbling, its paint cracked and peeling. The province of Nova Scotia bought it. Others—including schoolchildren—pitched in what was needed to pay the cost of taking it apart, restoring it, and rebuilding it, in 1998, inside the Art Gallery of Nova Scotia.

Complete with Maud's forget-me-not stairs, the house continues to cheer visitors from around the world each day. One child visiting the Maud Lewis exhibit said, "She painted what she saw, only she made it look better."

Among Maud's most famous customers were the Premier of Nova Scotia Robert Stanfield and U.S. President Richard Nixon. During Maud's lifetime her paintings sold for no more than ten dollars. In 2017, *Portrait of Eddie Barnes and Ed Murphy, Lobster Fishermen* sold for $45,000, and in 2022 *Black Truck* sold for $350,000. Three of Maud's paintings—*Winter Sleigh Ride*, *Team of Oxen in Winter*, and *Family and Sled*—have been featured on Canadian postage stamps. Maud never travelled more than an hour from home, but her paintings have been hung in galleries oceans away.

Author's Note

For many years I've enjoyed visiting my stepdaughter and her family in Nova Scotia. Gradually learning more about Maud Lewis—an artist the province is clearly, and rightly, proud of—I've been long enchanted by the colourful art she created.

Maud's house, itself a work of art, is such a wonderful expression of her talent, love of nature, sense of humour, and joy, I couldn't resist using words about it to frame this story, *A Tulip in Winter*.

The *Digby Courier* once said that Maud Lewis lived her life in a way that "shed beams of sunshine in the homes of others." Whatever your passions and whatever your challenges, I hope Maud's story will inspire you, in your own way, to do the same.

—Kathy Stinson

Illustrator's Note

When my husband and I moved to Nova Scotia over fifteen years ago, we bought a house that would have already been old in Maud's day, about half an hour away from where she spent most of her life. Her spirit is all around us here.

I've met many people who remember Maud personally. Few of them ever stopped at the side of the road and bought a painting. Sometimes we don't know the value of things until it's too late. But while Maud's work may not have always been valued during her lifetime, her fierce determination to make it, despite all hardships, left its mark on everyone who met her.

Everything Maud painted came from her own memories and imagination—a world filled with singing birds, long-lashed oxen, curious deer, blooming flowers, and fluffy cats. And that is what I have tried to recreate in the illustrations. A world with no shadows, just how she liked it.

I hope this book inspires you to notice the things that bring you joy and to find ways to share that joy with the rest of us.

—Lauren Soloy